Happy Fall & Winter!

Reproducible Activity Sheets for Grades K-1

Columbus Day
20

1
6
7
29
34
52
63
71

Same/Diff.
9 38
15
24

Troll Associates

Troll Teacher Time Savers provide a quick source of self-contained lessons and practice material, designed to be used as full-scale lessons or to make productive use of those precious extra minutes that sometimes turn up in the day's schedule.

Troll Teacher Time Savers can help you to prepare a made-to-order program for your students. Select the sequence of Time Savers that will meet your students' needs, and make as many photocopies of each page as you require. Since Time Savers include progressive levels of complexity and difficulty in each book, it is possible to individualize instruction, matching the needs of each student.

Those who need extra practice and reinforcement for catching up in their skills can benefit from Troll Teacher Time Savers, while other students can use Time Savers for enrichment or as a refresher for skills in which they haven't had recent practice. Time Savers can also be used to diagnose a student's knowledge and skills level, in order to see where extra practice is needed.

Time Savers can be used as homework assignments, classroom or small-group activities, shared learning with partners, or practice for standardized testing. See "Answer Key & Skills Index" to find the specific skill featured in each activity.

ANSWER KEY & SKILLS INDEX

Page 1, **My Monthly Calendar: (small-motor coordination)**

Page 2, **September: (small-motor coordination)**

Page 3, **Fall Months: (small-motor coordination)**

Page 4, **Puzzled on Labor Day:** Across, 2-hot; 3-parade; 4-milk; 6-beach; Down, 1-work; 2-hal; 3-picnic; 5-job. **(spelling)**

Page 5, **When You Grow Up: (social studies)**

Page 6, **New Friends: (counting)**

Page 7, **Going to School Maze: (maze)**

Page 8, **School Days:** 1-school; 2-books. **(spelling)**

Page 9, **Alike & Different: (same/different)**

Page 10, **Notebook Fun: (same/different)**

Page 11, **Show Him the Way: (maze)**

Page 12, **Put-Togethers: (matching)**

Page 13, **Busy Squirrel: (number sequencing)**

Page 14, **Catch a Leaf: (spelling)**

Page 15, **Falling Leaves: (same/different)**

Page 16, **Down Come the Leaves:** 1-leaves; 2-fall. **(spelling)**

Page 17, **First Day of Fall: (word recognition)**

Page 18, **October: (small-motor coordination)**

Page 19, **Columbus Day Maze: (maze)**

Page 20, **Your Own Discovery: (visual acuity)**

Page 21, **Columbus Day Count: (small-motor coordination)**

Page 22, **United Nations Day: (small-motor coordination)**

Page 23, **Pumpkin Puzzle: (spelling)**

Page 24, **What a Witch!: (same/different)**

Page 25, **Hungry Ghost: (number sequencing)**

Page 26, **Ghostly Alphabet:** 1-bat; 2-ghost; 3-Halloween; 4-pumpkin; 5-witch. **(alphabetizing)**

Page 27, **Monster Mask: (small-motor coordination)**

Page 28, **Halloween Opposites: (antonyms)**

My Monthly Calendar

Name _____

paste month here

Sunday	Monday	Tuesday	Wednesday	Thursday	Friday	Saturday

September

2

Paste-Ins

My Name _____

CUT AND GLUE THESE
PICTURES IN THE RIGHT
SPOTS ON YOUR CALENDAR

A GREAT DAY

A GREAT DAY

A GREAT DAY

A GREAT DAY

FULL MOON

ASTER

HAPPY BIRTHDAY!

HAPPY BIRTHDAY!

LABOR DAY

ROSH HASHANAH

BACK TO SCHOOL

INDIAN SUMMER

INDIAN SUMMER

FALL

CITIZENSHIP DAY

YOM KIPPUR

FIRST DAY OF FALL

SUNNY

SUNNY

CLOUDY

SUNNY

SUNNY

CLOUDY

SUNNY

SUNNY

CLOUDY

SUNNY

SUNNY

CLOUDY

RAIN

RAIN

RAIN

RAIN

RAIN

RAIN

WINDY

WINDY

WINDY

WINDY

WINDY

WINDY

 # Fall Months

GLUE
HERE

GLUE
HERE

GLUE
HERE

✂ CUT HERE

SEPTEMBER

OCTOBER

NOVEMBER

Color, cut
and glue
into the
right box.

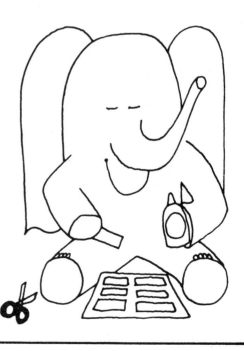

Name_____ **Date** _____

Puzzled on Labor Day

SQUAWK!

ACROSS

2. Is it cold or hot on Labor Day?
3. Sometimes you can see a Labor Day _ _ _ _ _ _ on T.V.
4. What do cows give?
6. On Labor Day lots of people sunbathe on the _ _ _ _ _ .

DOWN

1. Labor is another word for _ _ _ _ .
2. A huge animal found in the sea: w _ _ _ e.
3. Lots of people like to have a _ _ _ _ _ _ on Labor Day with lots of food.
4. Almost everyone who has a _ _ _ gets Labor Day off.

Name _____   Date _____

When You Grow Up

Labor Day is a day of rest for people who work all year long. Where would you like to work someday? Draw a picture of the job you'd like to have.

Name_____ **Date** _____

5

New Friends

How many girls are
in this class?   _____

How many boys are
in this class?   _____

How many children are in this
class altogether?   _____

Going to School Maze

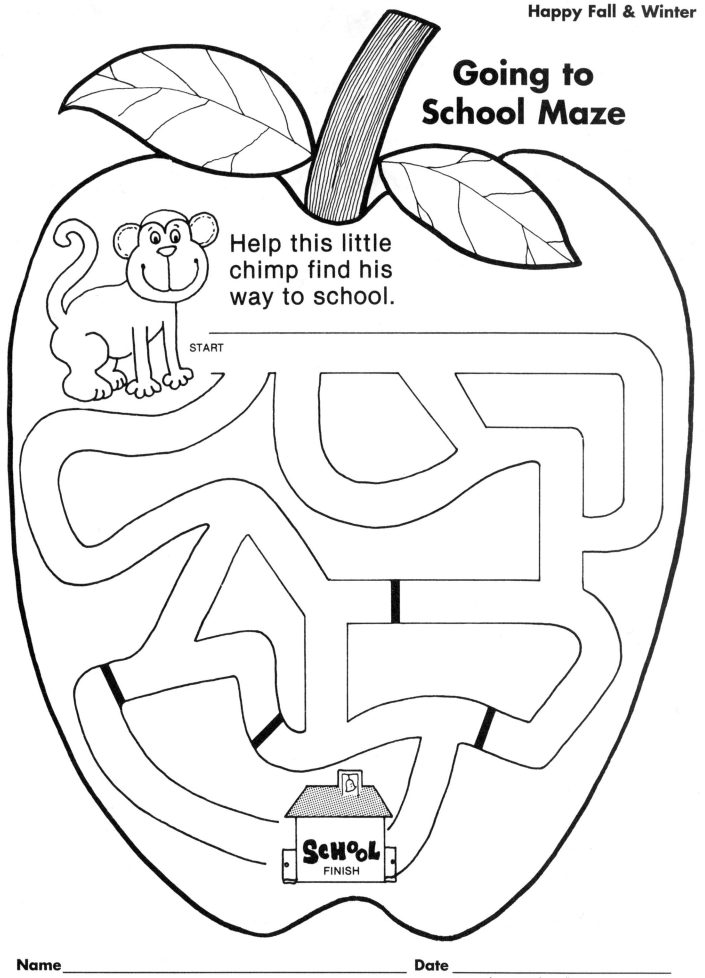

Help this little chimp find his way to school.

START

SCHOOL
FINISH

Name_____

Date _____

School Days

ACROSS

1. Place where children go to learn.

DOWN

2. In school we read lots of b _ _ _ _ .

2. B

1. S

Name_____ **Date**_____

8

Alike & Different

Put an X on the object that
looks different in each row.

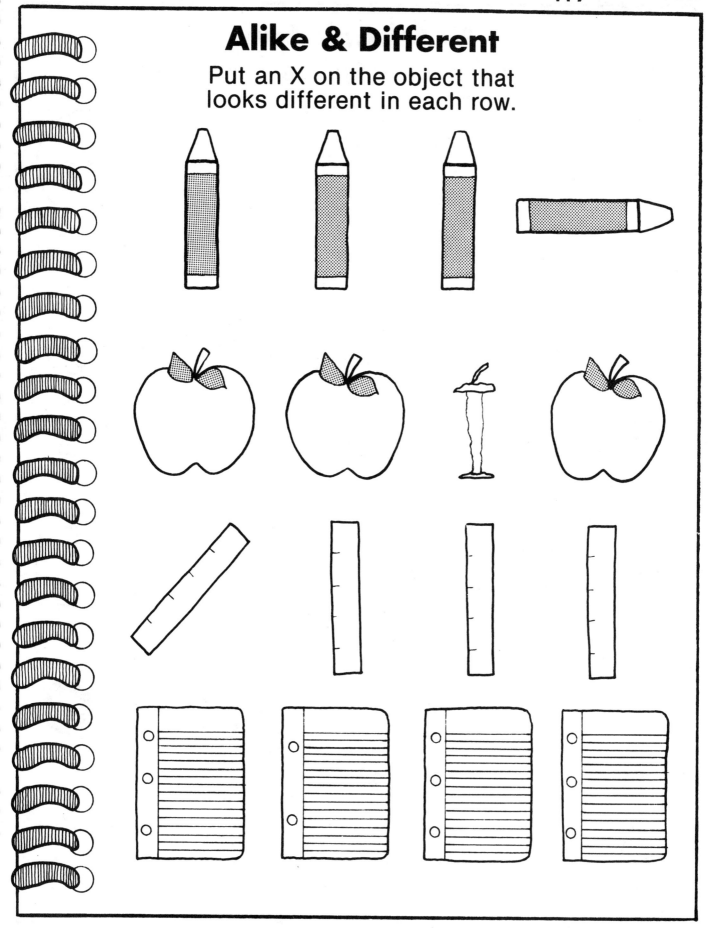

Name_____ **Date** _____

Notebook Fun
Number these in order from smallest to largest.

 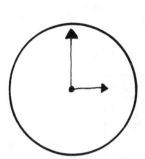 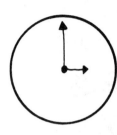

_____ _____ _____ _____

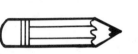 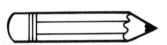 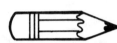

_____ _____ _____ _____

_____ _____ _____ _____

_____ _____ _____ _____

Name_____ **Date**_____

Show Him the Way

Help Oliver Owl find his friend Orson.

START

Oliver

FINISH

Orson

Name_____ Date_____

11

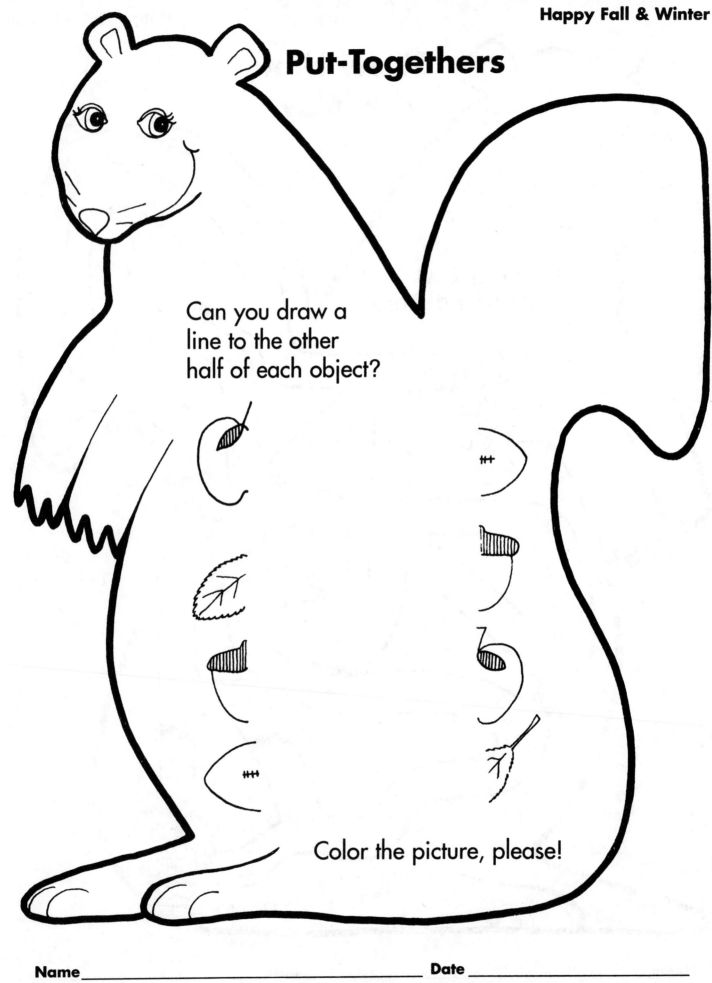

Put-Togethers

Can you draw a line to the other half of each object?

Color the picture, please!

Name _____

Date _____

Busy Squirrel

What is the squirrel's favorite food? Connect the dots to find out!

Name_____ **Date**_____

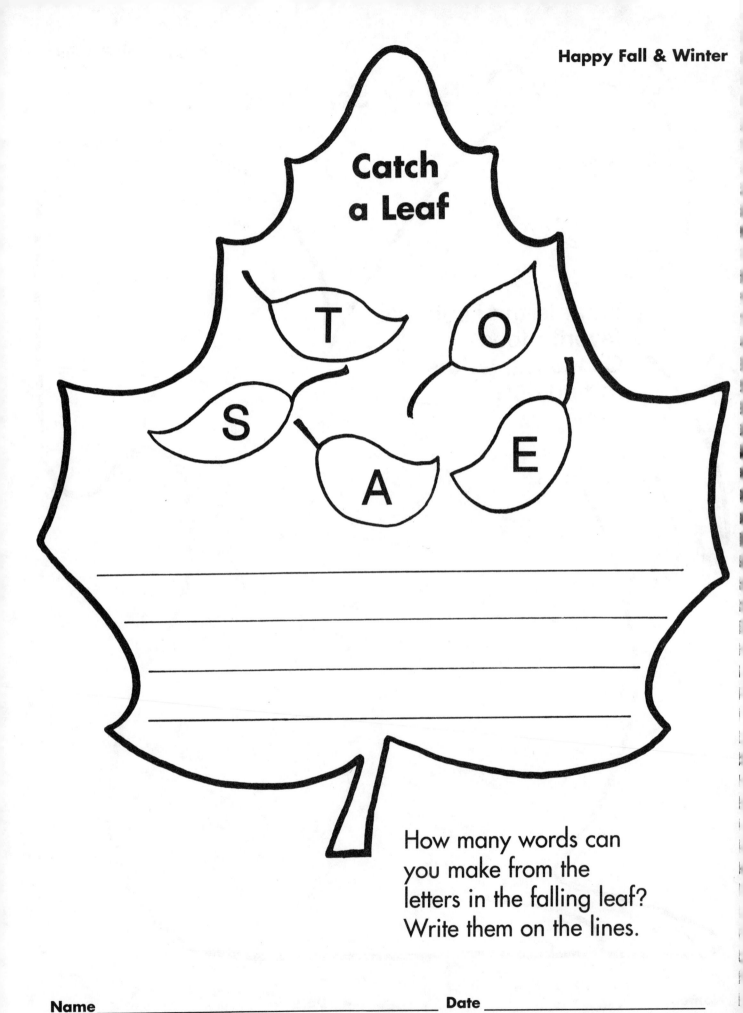

Happy Fall & Winter

Catch
a Leaf

T
O
S
A
E

How many words can
you make from the
letters in the falling leaf?
Write them on the lines.

Name_____ Date_____

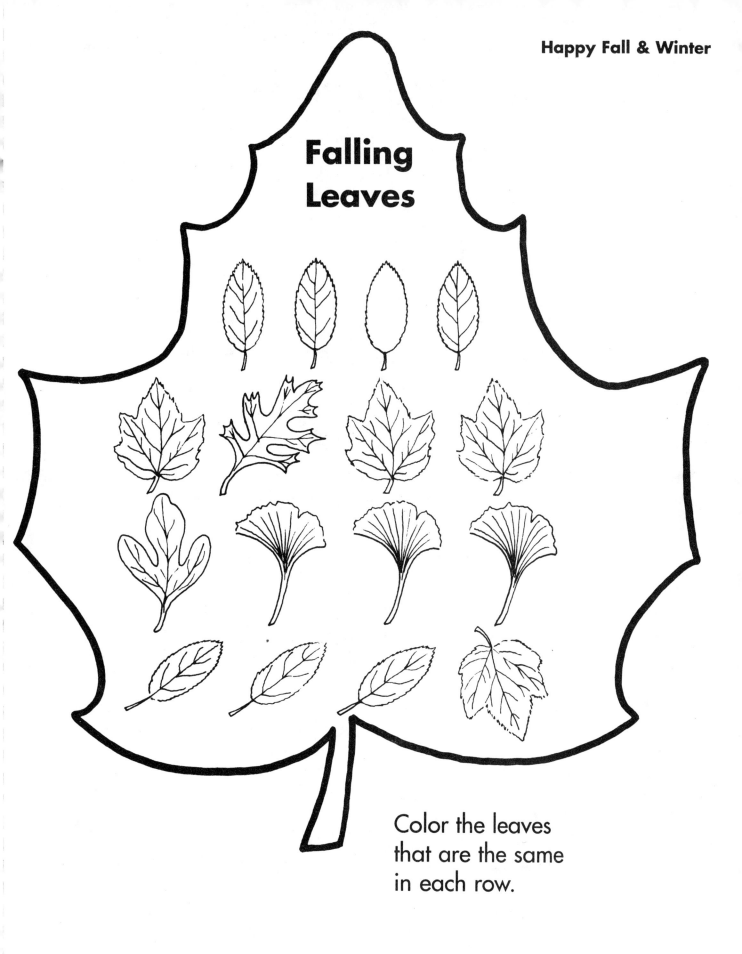

Happy Fall & Winter

Falling Leaves

Color the leaves
that are the same
in each row.

Down Come the Leaves

ACROSS

1. It's fun to collect all kinds of _____ in the fall.

DOWN

2. The season before winter is _____.

Name_____

Date_____

16

 # First Day of Fall

The first day of fall is usually September 22nd or 23rd. The Earth has traveled a quarter of its way around the sun. Here is a Fall puzzle for you to do. Find each of these words in the puzzle. Look across and down. One is done for you.

A	P	P	L	E	R
U	L	L	O	N	A
T	R	E	E	D	K
U	U	A	N	J	E
M	V	F	A	L	L
N	W	I	N	D	Y

APPLE
AUTUMN
TREE
WINDY
RAKE
LEAF
FALL

Name_____ Date _____

October

Paste-Ins

CALENDULA

HAPPY BIRTHDAY!

HAPPY BIRTHDAY!

HAPPY BIRTHDAY!

A GREAT DAY

A GREAT DAY

A GREAT DAY

A GREAT DAY

FULL MOON

CUT AND GLUE THESE
PICTURES IN THE RIGHT
SPOTS ON YOUR CALENDAR

COLUMBUS DAY

HALLOWEEN PUMPKIN

HALLOWEEN GHOST

HALLOWEEN WITCH

SUNNY

SUNNY

SUNNY

SUNNY

SUNNY

SUNNY

LEAVES

LEAVES

LEAVES

LEAVES

WINDY

WINDY

WINDY

WINDY

WINDY

WINDY

CLOUDY

CLOUDY

CLOUDY

CLOUDY

CLOUDY

SNOW

SNOW

RAIN

RAIN

RAIN

RAIN

RAIN

RAIN

18

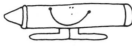

Columbus Day Maze

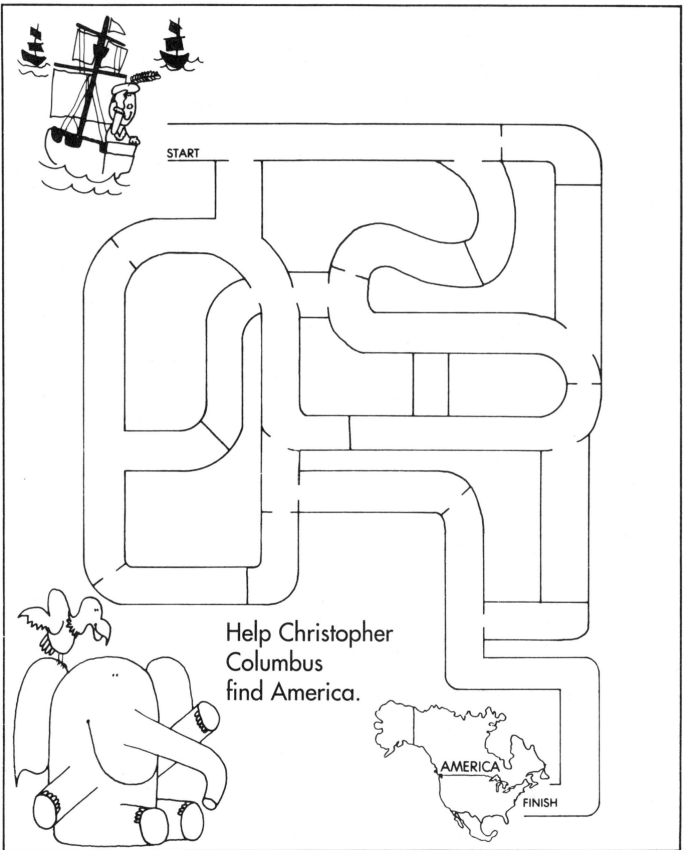

START

Help Christopher
Columbus
find America.

AMERICA

FINISH

Name_____ **Date** _____

19

 # Your Own Discovery

How many boats can
you find in this picture?
Color each one.

Name_____   **Date** _____

Columbus Day Count

CUT HERE

How many ships did Columbus sail to the New World? Cut and glue them in the water, and color the picture.

NINA

PINTA

SANTA MARIA

Name _____ Date _____

21

United Nations Day

United Nations Day is October 24. It is the birthday of the United Nations. In the U.N., countries work for peace in the world.

Here is a dove, the bird of peace, that you can make.

1. Cut out the rectangle.

2. Fold it in half.

3. Cut out the bird.

4. Fold out the wings.

5. Punch a hole and hang in your window with string.

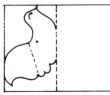

1. CUT HERE   2. FOLD HERE

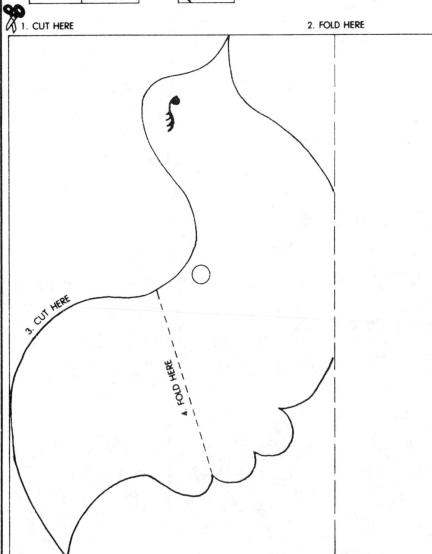

3. CUT HERE

4. FOLD HERE

Name_____   **Date** _____

Pumpkin Puzzle

Halloween is Coming!

a	t	b
c	t	a
o	b	o

This pumpkin has mixed up his words. See if you can unscramble them.

Name_____   Date_____

23

Copyright © 1996 by Troll Communications L.L.C.

What a Witch

Halloween is Coming!

Color the witches that are the same in each row.

Name_____ **Date** _____

24

Hungry Ghost

BOooo!

16   17   18   2   3

15   1   4

14   5

13   6

12   7

11   9   8
10

Connect the dots to see what this ghost ate for a snack.

Name_____   Date_____

25

Ghostly Alphabet

BOooo!

Put these Halloween words in alphabetical order.

Halloween

1. _____

ghost

2. _____

pumpkin

3. _____

bat

4. _____

witch

5. _____

Name_____ **Date** _____

26

 # Monster Mask

Make your own monster mask! Color and cut out the eyes, nose, and mouth below. Glue them on a paper bag and wear it over your head.

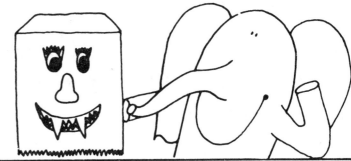

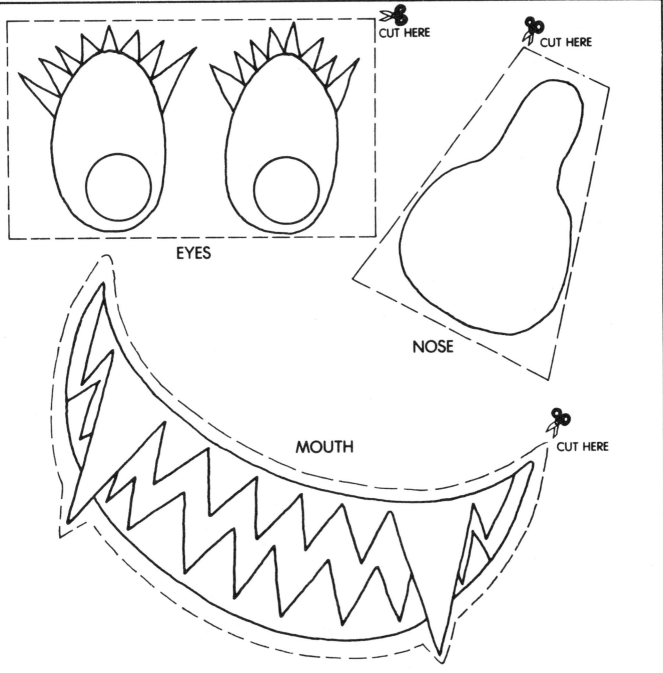

CUT HERE

CUT HERE

EYES

NOSE

MOUTH   CUT HERE

Name _____   **Date** _____

27

Halloween Opposites

Write the opposite of each word below. Let the Halloween characters help you.

 happy  _____

 cold 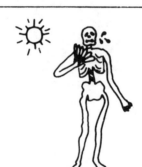 _____

 short  _____

 thin  _____

Name_____ **Date** _____

28

Guess Who's a Ghost?

Who could this be?
Write the name of
the animal on the line.

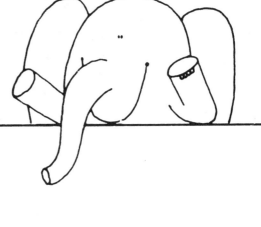

_____
_____

_____
_____

_____
_____

_____
_____

Name_____ **Date** _____

29

Trick-or-Treat Bag

Color and cut out these Halloween shapes. Glue them on a bag with a handle on it. Now you have your own Trick-or-Treat bag!

BOO!

CUT HERE

Name_____ Date _____

November

My Name _____

Paste-Ins

SUNNY · SUNNY · CLOUDY · ELECTION DAY · A GREAT DAY · A GREAT DAY

A GREAT DAY · CHRYSANTHEMUM

SUNNY · SUNNY · CLOUDY · VETERANS DAY · A GREAT DAY · FULL MOON

HAPPY BIRTHDAY!

SUNNY · SUNNY · CLOUDY · THANKSGIVING DAY · A GREAT DAY

HAPPY BIRTHDAY!

SUNNY · SUNNY · CLOUDY · THANKSGIVING DAY

RAIN · RAIN · RAIN · THANKSGIVING DAY

RAIN · RAIN · RAIN · SCARF

CUT AND GLUE THESE PICTURES IN THE RIGHT SPOTS ON YOUR CALENDAR

WINDY · WINDY · MITTENS · SNOW

WINDY · WINDY · HAT · SNOW · SNOW

 # Sleepy Squirrel

What is this squirrel doing?

_____

Cut out the square. Color the squirrel and his tail. Fold the square on the dotted line. Cut and paste the tail where shown. Then go over the broken lines and write the word *squirrel.*

✂ CUT HERE

FOLD
HERE

squirrel

PASTE HERE

Name_____ **Date** _____

Time to Vote

Put an X next to whom you want to be President, Elmo or Dudley. Count the animals on each side and add your vote. Who has more votes? Who won?

My Ballot

Name_____

_____

Vote for one

Elmo Elephant ☐

Dudley Donkey ☐

Veteran's Day Paper Whistle

Cut the whistle out along solid black line.

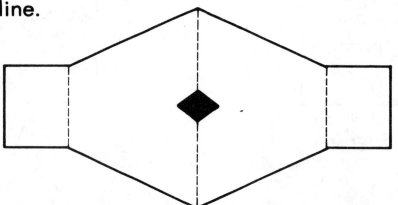

Fold in ½ along the middle dotted line.

Cut out ◆ on dotted fold line.

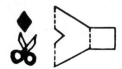

Fold each end flap toward the middle on dotted lines.

Bend out flaps slightly.

Hold to your mouth and blow *gently*.

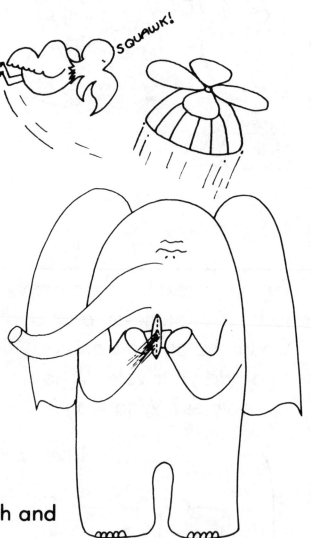

SQUAWK!

Veteran's Day March

Another name for a VETERAN is a SOLDIER. Soldiers march LEFT RIGHT LEFT RIGHT. Which way are these soldiers marching?

⟵▭ left   right ▭⟶

_____
_ _ _ _ _ _ _ _ _ _ _ _ _
_____

_____
_ _ _ _ _ _ _ _ _ _ _ _ _
_____

_____
_ _ _ _ _ _ _ _ _ _ _ _ _
_____

_____
_ _ _ _ _ _ _ _ _ _ _ _ _
_____

Name_____   **Date** _____

35

Thanksgiving Fun

The Indians showed the Pilgrims how to plant corn and squash. The Pilgrims had a party with the Indians. They gave thanks for the food and their new home.

What are you thankful for?

_____

_____

_____

Color this
Thanksgiving picture.

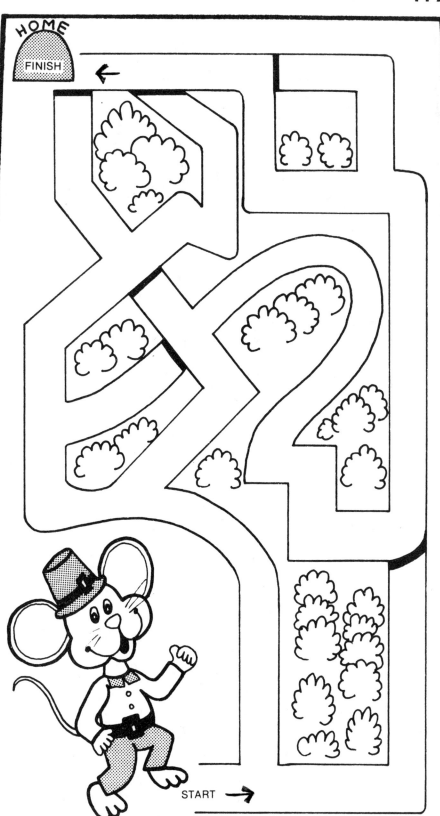

HOME
FINISH

Thanksgiving

Maze

START →

This little mouse is almost late for Thanksgiving dinner.
Help him find his way back home.

Name_____ Date _____

37

Put an X on the object that
is different in each row.

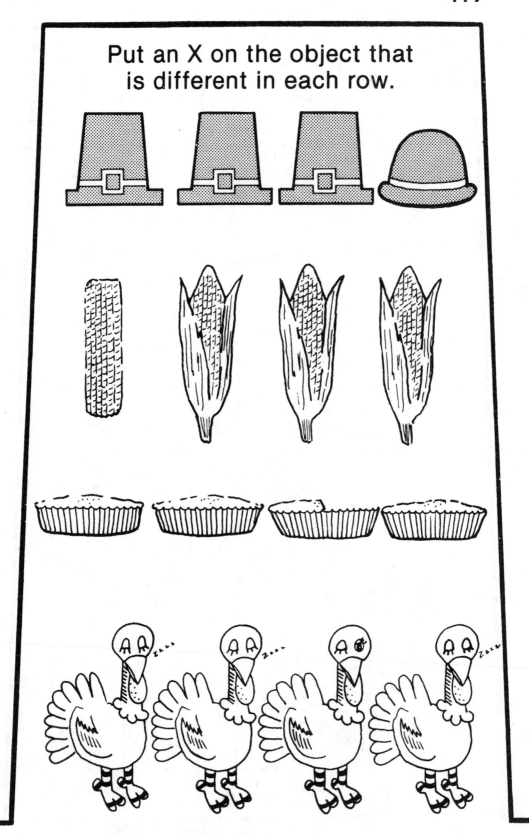

Thanksgiving Time

Name_____ Date _____

Turkey Hunt

Can you find these words?
Circle them.

turkey   corn   pumpkin   thanks   eat   top   fun   on

G F A J E A T
T U R K E Y H
O N H I Q H A
P U M P K I N
K S V O M A K
T C O R N B S

The first one is done for you.

Name_____   **Date** _____

39

Word Bird

Draw lines to join the words that rhyme.

meat   tie

pie   cat

car   seat

hat   star

Name _____ Date _____

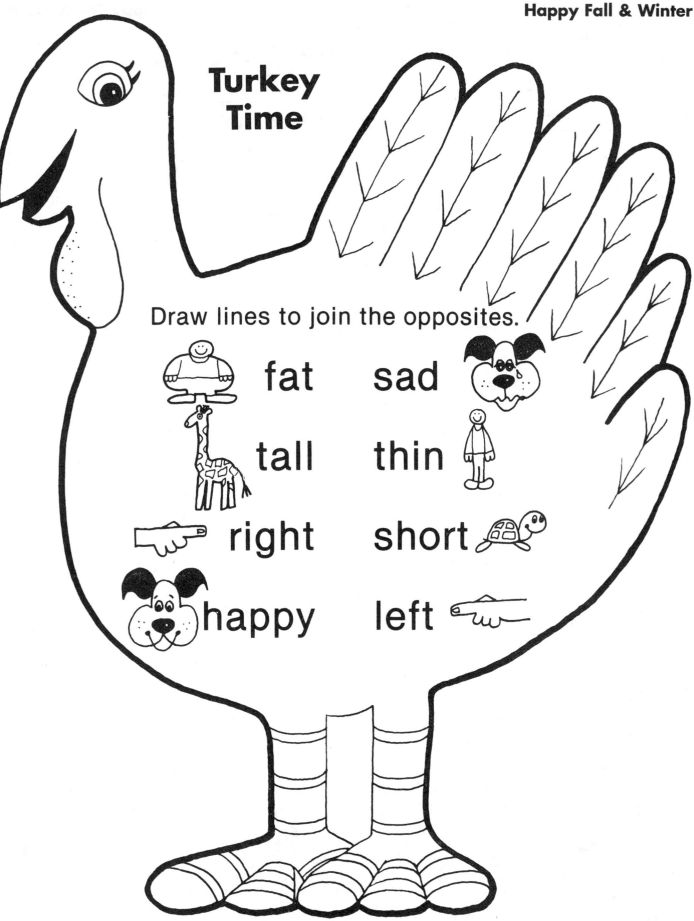

Turkey Time

Draw lines to join the opposites.

fat   sad

tall   thin

right   short

happy   left

Name_____   Date_____

Cut & Paste Shopping Fun

Color the food that you want to buy for Thanksgiving dinner. Then cut out and glue the pictures in the shopping cart.

CUT HERE

PINEAPPLE · TURKEY · CEREAL · CRANBERRY JELLY · PEAS · STUFFING

CORN ON THE COB · HAMBURGER · SWEET POTATOES · CARROTS · MILK · EGGS

Name _____ Date _____

Happy Fall & Winter

Color & Cut Place Cards

Make your own place cards for Thanksgiving dinner. Color and cut out cards on solid black lines. Fold in half along dotted lines.

CUT HERE

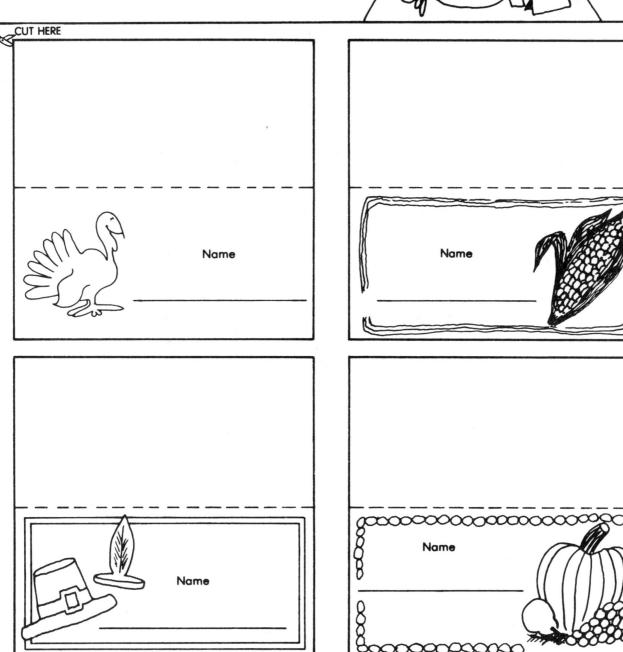

Name_____ Date _____

43

Copyright © 1996 by Troll Communications L.L.C.

 # Thanksgiving Puzzler

Find each of these 7 words in the puzzle.
Look across and down. One is done for you.

S	T	V	B	T	R	T
Q	J	U	A	U	G	H
L	M	C	O	R	N	A
P	U	M	P	K	I	N
Z	F	K	A	E	H	K
C	O	I	E	Y	T	S
G	O	B	B	L	E	J
A	D	F	E	A	S	T

PUMPKIN
TURKEY
FOOD
GOBBLE
THANKS
CORN
FEAST

 # Winter Months

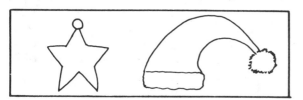

GLUE
HERE

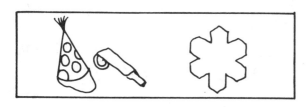

GLUE
HERE

GLUE
HERE

CUT HERE

DECEMBER

JANUARY Happy New Year!

FEBRUARY

Color, cut, and glue into the right box.

Name _____ Date _____

45

December

My Name

Paste-Ins

CUT AND GLUE THESE
PICTURES IN THE RIGHT
SPOTS ON YOUR CALENDAR

A GREAT DAY

A GREAT DAY

A GREAT DAY

A GREAT DAY

FULL MOON

POINSETTIA

HAPPY BIRTHDAY

HAPPY BIRTHDAY

WINDY

CLOUDY

KWANZAA BEGINS

HANUKKAH BEGINS

WINDY

CLOUDY

SUNNY

WINTER BEGINS

WINDY

CLOUDY

SUNNY

CHRISTMAS

WINDY

CLOUDY

SUNNY

NEW YEAR'S EVE

SNOW

SNOW

SLEDDING

SNOW

SNOW

RAIN

MITTENS

SNOW

MITTENS

RAIN

SNOW

HAT

SNOW

CLOUDY

SLEDDING

SNOW

SNOW

46

Color the candles that are the same in each row.

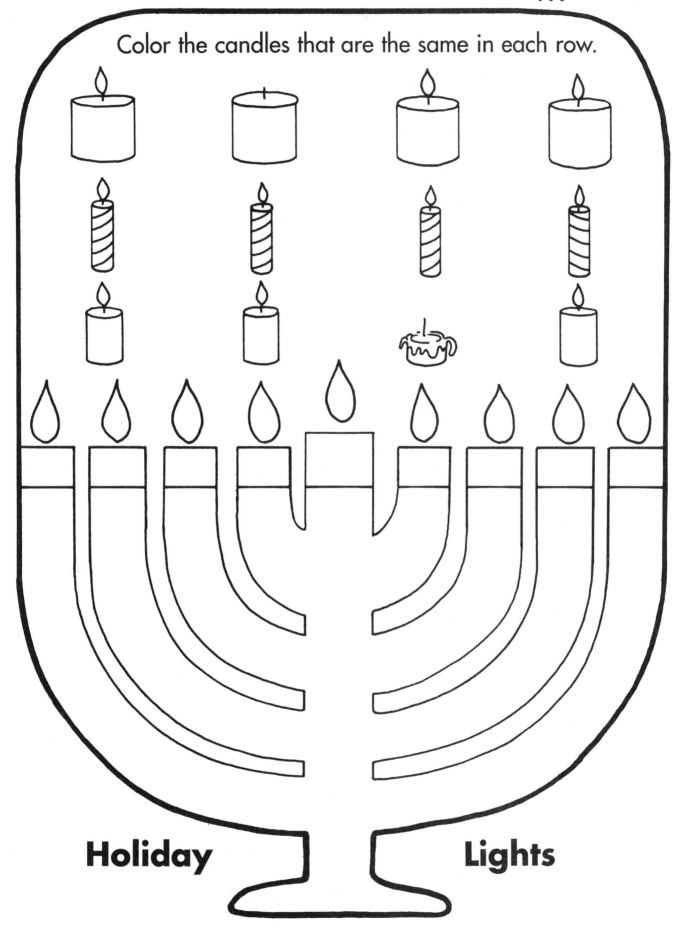

Holiday   **Lights**

Name _____   **Date** _____

Holiday Gift Tags

Here are 8 holiday tags that you can use for gifts. Color the design on each one. Cut out on the dotted line. Fasten to gift with tape.

CUT HERE

To
_____
From
_____

To
_____
From
_____

To
_____
From
_____

To
_____
From
_____

To
_____
From
_____

To
_____
From
_____

To
_____
From
_____

To
_____
From
_____

Name_____   **Date**_____

48

Happy Hanukkah

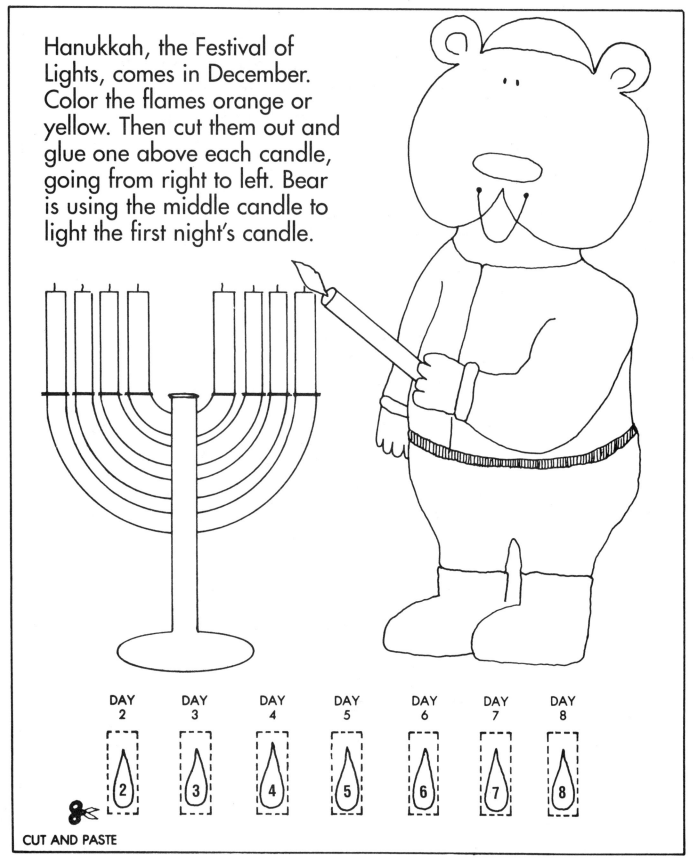

Hanukkah, the Festival of Lights, comes in December. Color the flames orange or yellow. Then cut them out and glue one above each candle, going from right to left. Bear is using the middle candle to light the first night's candle.

DAY 2 DAY 3 DAY 4 DAY 5 DAY 6 DAY 7 DAY 8

2   3   4   5   6   7   8

CUT AND PASTE

Name_____ Date_____

 # First Day of Winter

The first day of winter is usually December 21st or 22nd.
That is the shortest day of the year. Here is a winter puzzle
for you to do. Find each of these 7 words in the puzzle.
Draw circles around them. Look across and down.
One is done for you.

S	L	E	D	L	R
U	K	S	K	I	X
W	I	N	T	E	R
I	C	O	L	D	G
C	A	W	O	J	N
E	W	H	I	T	E

SNOW
WINTER
SLED
SKI
COLD
ICE
WHITE

Name_____ Date _____

Winter Maze

Help this skating reindeer find his sleigh full of little friends.

START

FINISH

Name _____ Date _____

 # Holiday Stars

CUT HERE

1. Cut out the square below.

2. Fold square in half.

3. Fold in half again.

4. Fold in half so it looks like a triangle.

5. Fold triangle in half again.

6. Open up paper. Lie flat.

7. Fold each of the 4 corners under.

8. Push in where shown.

9. Now you have a star. Punch a hole in the top and hang it in your window.

Name _____

Date _____

 # Finger Puppets

Gingerbread people make fun finger puppets for Christmas. Color the first one. Then draw your own face and clothes on the second one. Cut them both out and tape the tabs around your two fingers. Can you think of a story about the gingerbread people?

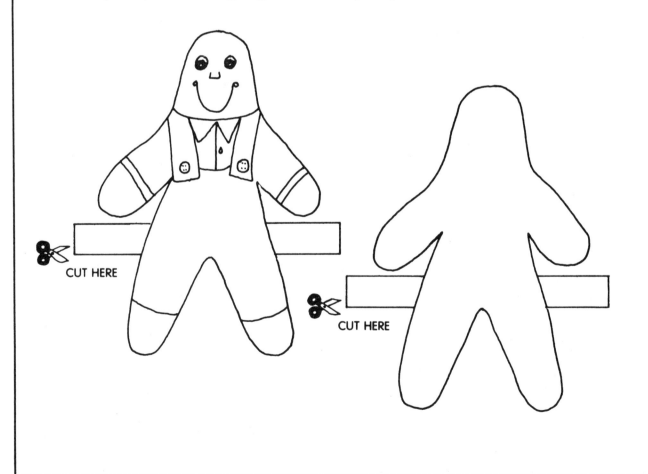

CUT HERE

CUT HERE

Name_____ Date_____

53

Time to Trim the Tree

Can you decorate this Christmas tree? Don't forget a star at the top.

Name_____ **Date**_____

54

Christmas Puzzler

Find each of these 8 words in the puzzle. Draw circles around them. Look across and down. One is done for you.

S	A	N	T	A	R	H
T	R	E	E	U	G	O
O	M	C	O	E	N	L
C	A	N	D	L	E	I
K	F	K	A	F	H	D
I	O	S	T	A	R	A
N	O	P	B	L	E	Y
G	R	I	B	B	O	N

SANTA
STOCKING
TREE
CANDLE
HOLIDAY
RIBBON
STAR
ELF

Name_____ **Date**_____

Count & Color

Here are some small Santas. Color their hats red. How many small Santas are there?

_____

Name_____ Date_____

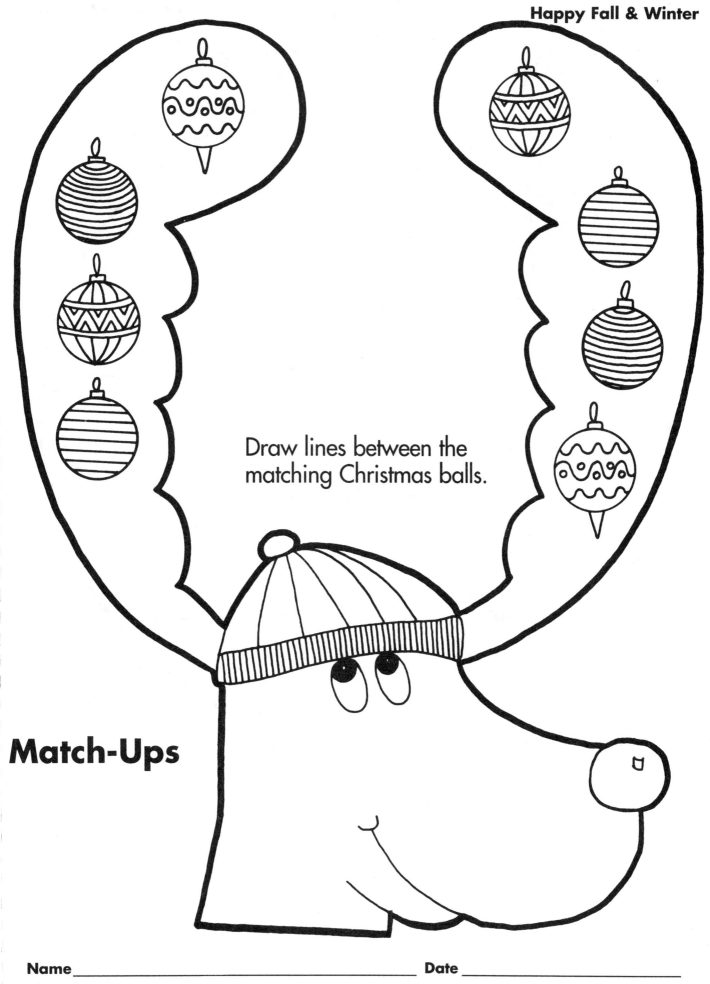

Draw lines between the matching Christmas balls.

Match-Ups

Name_____   Date_____

Alphabet   Fun

Put these Christmas words
in alphabetical order.

 Santa 1._____

 gift 2._____

 angel 3._____

train 4._____

Name_____ Date _____

58

Let's Celebrate Kwanzaa

Kwanzaa is a holiday that honors African American people and their past. "Kwanzaa" means first fruits of the harvest in Swahili. Swahili is a language spoken in East Africa.

Part of celebrating Kwanzaa is remembering ancestors. Write down the names of as many of your ancestors, or relatives, as you can.

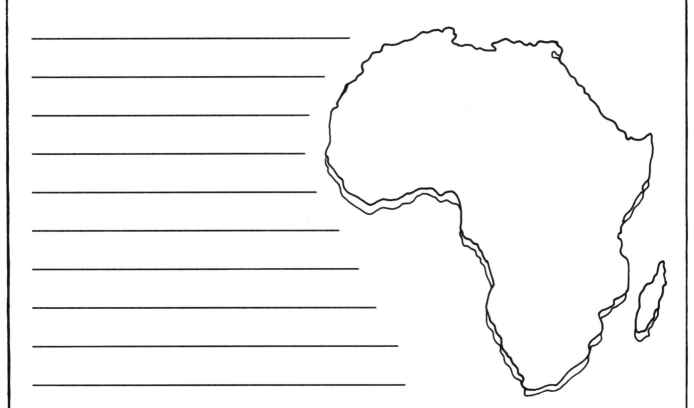

_____

_____

_____

_____

_____

_____

_____

_____

The Swahili word for calling out the names of ancestors is "kukumbuka." Call out the names of your ancestors to thank them for giving you life.

Color the Kinara

A Kinara is a special candelabra that holds the seven candles lit during Kwanzaa. The seven candles stand for the seven principles of the holiday, unity, community, pride, cooperation, creativity, purpose, faith.

Do the addition problems in the candles. Then color the Kinara.

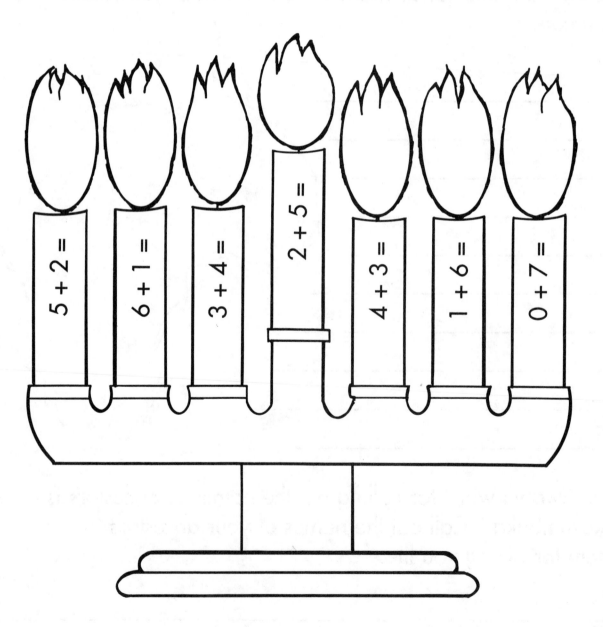

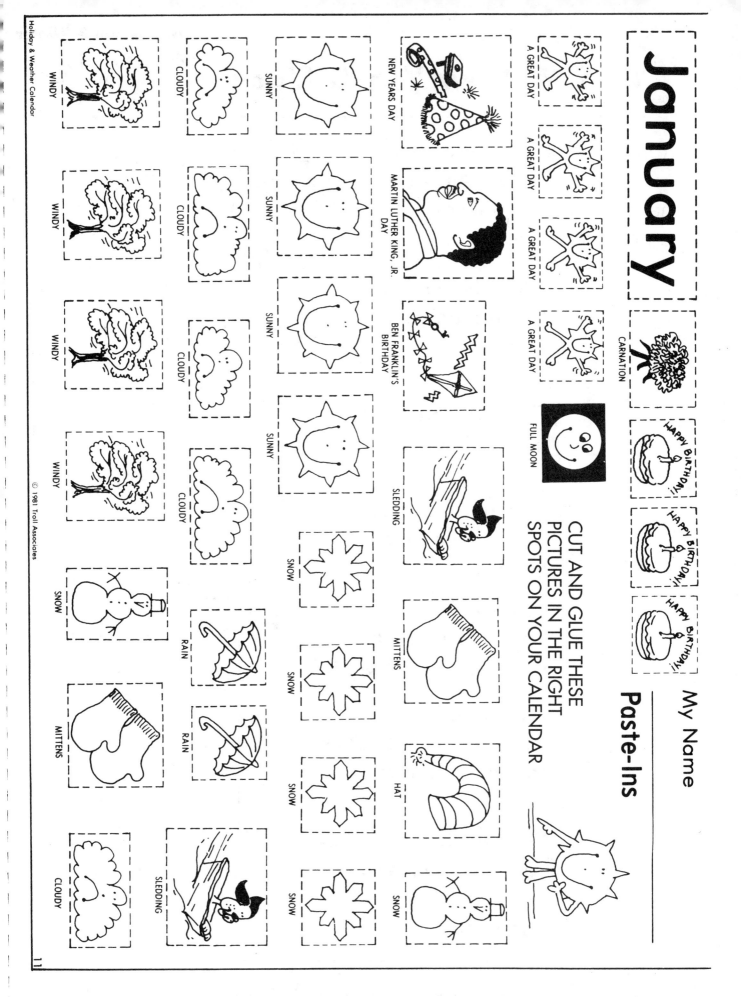

January

My Name

Paste-Ins

CUT AND GLUE THESE
PICTURES IN THE RIGHT
SPOTS ON YOUR CALENDAR

New Year's Clock

You can make your own clock for New Year's Eve. All you need is a paper plate and a paper fastener.

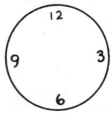

Write the numbers, like this, on your plate.

Then add the rest of the numbers 1–12.

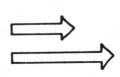

Cut out the big hand and little hand from this sheet.

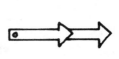

Push the paper fastener through the hands where shown. (X)

Then push it through the center of your clock. Fasten the fastener in back.

Move the hands so they both point to the 12. What time is it now? Happy New Year!

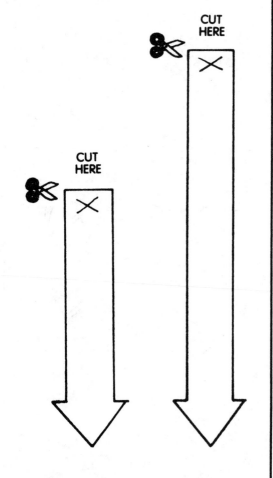

CUT HERE

CUT HERE

How many snowmen have hats? _____

How many have brooms? _____

How many are smiling? _____

Snowmen Fun

Remembering Martin Luther King, Jr.

Martin Luther King, Jr. wanted all Americans to have the same rights. He wanted all people to be treated fairly. He led a march to Washington, D.C., so that poor people might have a chance for a better life.

Martin Luther King, Jr. gave a speech in Washington and talked about his hopes for the future.

Look at the words.
Color the letter **I** green.
Color the letter **M** brown.
Color the letter **E** red.
Color the letter **A** blue.
Color the letter **H** pink.
Color the letter **R** black.
Color the letter **V** yellow.
Color the letter **D** purple.

I HAVE A DREAM

Name_____ **Date**_____

March for Justice

Martin Luther King, Jr. helped workers fight for better lives. He often led marches to show the unity of the workers.

Count the people behind Martin Luther King, Jr. _____

How many people are carrying signs? _____

How many people are wearing hats? _____

Name_____ **Date**_____

65

February

My Name _____

Paste-Ins

CUT AND GLUE THESE
PICTURES IN THE RIGHT
SPOTS ON YOUR CALENDAR

A GREAT DAY

A GREAT DAY

A GREAT DAY

A GREAT DAY

VIOLET

FULL MOON

HAPPY BIRTHDAY!

HAPPY BIRTHDAY!

HAPPY BIRTHDAY!

ABRAHAM LINCOLN'S BIRTHDAY

ST. VALENTINE'S DAY

GEORGE WASHINGTON'S BIRTHDAY

GROUND-HOG DAY

SLEDDING

HAT

MITTENS

SNOW

SNOW

SNOW

SNOW

SNOW

SNOW

WINDY

WINDY

WINDY

SUNNY

SUNNY

SUNNY

SUNNY

SUNNY

RAIN

RAIN

CLOUDY

CLOUDY

CLOUDY

CLOUDY

CLOUDY

SLEDDING

MITTENS

66

Sleeping Animals

What is this ground hog doing? _____
Animals who sleep during the winter are HIBERNATING.
Before they sleep they store enough food for the winter months.

Cut out the square below. Color the ground hog. Then
write the word **ground hog**. Fold the square
along the dotted line and stand it on your shelf.

CUT HERE

FOLD
HERE

ground hog

Name _____   **Date** _____

Puzzled on Ground-Hog Day

Here is a puzzle about some Ground-Hog Day beliefs.

ACROSS

2. If it is cloudy on Feb. 2 then _ _ _ _ _ _ is coming.
3. Feb. 2 is Ground-Hog _ _ _ .
4. If it is sunny on Feb. 2, then there will be 6 more weeks of _ _ _ _ _ _ .

DOWN

1. The ground hog lives under the _ _ _ _ _ _ _ .
2. When a ground hog sees his _ _ _ _ _ _ _ , there will be 6 more weeks of winter.
5. The ground hog has a furry coat to keep him _ _ _ _ .

Abraham Lincoln

 # Abraham Lincoln

Abraham Lincoln's birthday is February 12th.
He was the 16th President of the United States.
He was known as Honest Abe.

Abraham Lincoln's picture is on a penny.
True or False?   T   F

How many pennies are here?   _____

Abraham Lincoln lived
in a palace.
True or False?   T   F

Draw Abraham Lincoln's house.
Color it.

Abraham Lincoln wore a clown hat.
True or False?   T   F

Cut and glue the hat Abraham Lincoln wore.

   CUT HERE

PASTE HERE

Name_____   Date_____

69

Copyright © 1996 by Troll Communications L.L.C.

Valentine Look-Alikes

Circle the object in each row
that is like the first one on
the left.

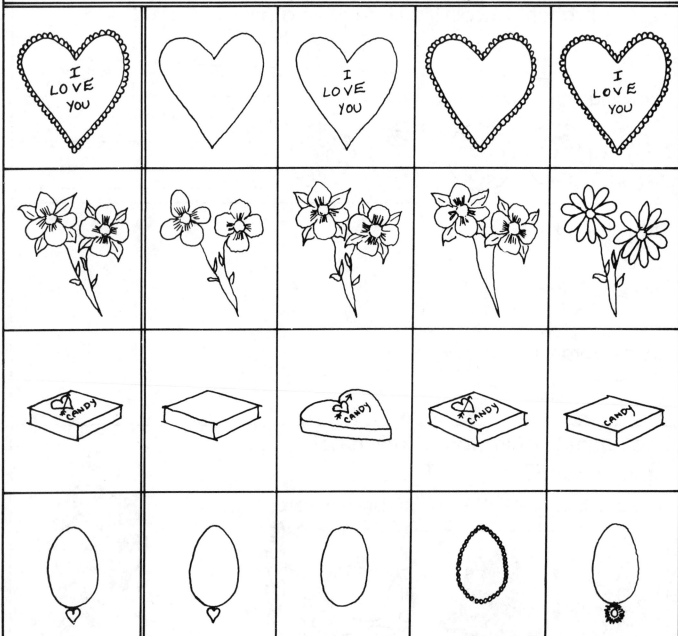

Name_____   Date _____

 # Hiding Hearts

How many hearts can you
find in the picture below?
Color each one red.

Name_____ Date _____

 # Valentine Match-Ups

Which ones go together?
Look at the first picture
in each row. Circle the
picture that matches it.

Valentine Cards

Color the cards below.
Be sure to use some red.
Cut the cards out and
give them to your friends!

CUT HERE

Be my valentine

Please be mine!

From your secret admirer

You are the 1 for me!

Name_____ **Date**_____

73

Copyright © 1996 by Troll Communications L.L.C.

What Comes Next?

Cut out and paste the number in the box on each picture to show what happened 1st, 2nd, 3rd and 4th.

Name _____

Date _____

Washington's Birthday

George Washington was the first president of the United States. People celebrate his birthday on the 3rd Monday in February. His picture is on a one dollar bill.

Below, color and cut out the picture you think is George Washington. Then glue it on the one dollar bill.

CUT HERE

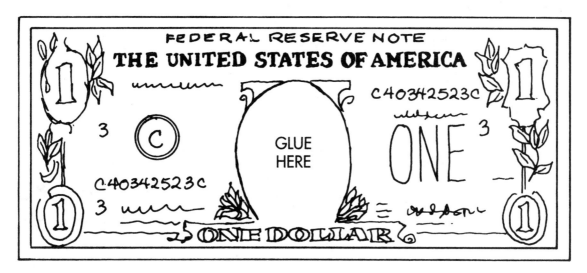

FEDERAL RESERVE NOTE
THE UNITED STATES OF AMERICA
C40342523C
3 C
GLUE HERE
ONE 3
C40342523C
3
ONE DOLLAR

Name_____ Date_____

Hurrah, Mr. President!

George Washington was a hero of the American Revolution and our first president. When he was finished being president, he returned to Mount Vernon, his home in Virginia.

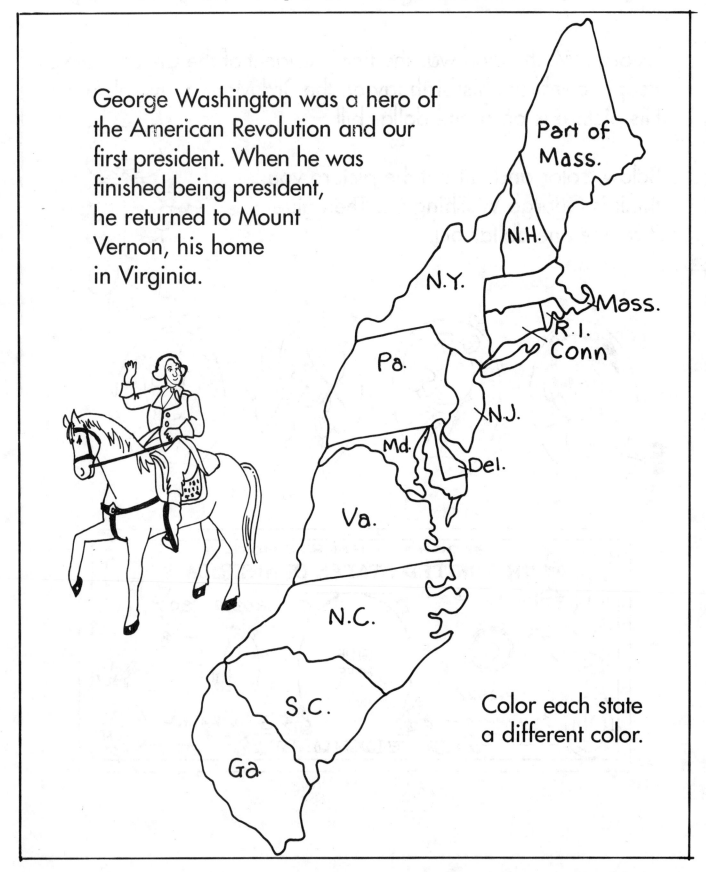

Color each state a different color.